ANIMAL SURVIVAL

GETTING SMELLY TO SURVIVE

BY CLARA MacCARALD

CONTENT CONSULTANT
CHRISTINE DREA, PhD
DEPARTMENT OF EVOLUTIONARY ANTHROPOLOGY
DEPARTMENT OF BIOLOGY
DUKE UNIVERSITY

Kids Core

An Imprint of Abdo Publishing
abdobooks.com

abdobooks.com

Published by Abdo Publishing, a division of ABDO, PO Box 398166, Minneapolis, Minnesota 55439. Copyright © 2023 by Abdo Consulting Group, Inc. International copyrights reserved in all countries. No part of this book may be reproduced in any form without written permission from the publisher. Kids Core™ is a trademark and logo of Abdo Publishing.

Printed in the United States of America, North Mankato, Minnesota.
052022
092022

THIS BOOK CONTAINS
RECYCLED MATERIALS

Cover Photo: Jemini Joseph/Shutterstock Images
Interior Photos: Martin Harvey/Science Source, 4–5; Arend van der Walt/Shutterstock Images, 6; Matt Jeppson/Shutterstock Images, 7; Claudia Paulussen/Shutterstock Images, 8; Debbie Steinhausser/Shutterstock Images, 10–11, 28 (bottom); Red Line Editorial, 13; Wild Media/Shutterstock Images, 15, 28 (top); Shutterstock Images, 16–17, 18, 29 (top); iStockphoto, 20; F. Hecker/Blick Winkel/Alamy, 22–23, 29 (bottom); Evgeniy Andreev/iStockphoto, 24; Martin Hejzlar/Shutterstock Images, 25; Roger Wissmann/Shutterstock Images, 26

Editor: Ann Schwab
Series Designer: Katharine Hale

Library of Congress Control Number: 2021951724

Publisher's Cataloging-in-Publication Data

Names: MacCarald, Clara, author.
Title: Getting smelly to survive / by Clara MacCarald
Description: Minneapolis, Minnesota : Abdo Publishing, 2023 | Series: Animal survival | Includes online resources and index.
Identifiers: ISBN 9781532198502 (lib. bdg.) | ISBN 9781644947678 (pbk.) | ISBN 9781098272159 (ebook)
Subjects: LCSH: Animal defenses--Juvenile literature. | Defense measures--Juvenile literature. | Adaptation (Physiology)--Juvenile literature. | Animal behavior--Juvenile literature.
Classification: DDC 591.57--dc23

CONTENTS

The striped polecat hunts small animals such as rats, mice, and frogs.

CHAPTER 1

THE POWER OF SMELL

Under a starry sky in a dark African grassland, a striped polecat moves along the brush. The polecat, also known as a Zorilla, is searching for food. It senses movement in the grass. Suddenly, a jackal leaps toward the polecat.

A jackal hunts for prey in the African grassland.

The polecat tries to run, but the **predator** is too close. A terrible stink fills the jackal's nose. It's coming from **glands** in the polecat's rear. The jackal remembers that smell. It knows that next

Playing Dead

Some animals use smell as just one part of a survival plan. Hognose snakes go belly-up. This makes them appear dead. The snakes can make this act appear more real by adding an awful smell.

Hognose snakes are among the many animals that use odor to keep predators from eating them.

the polecat would spray the jackal's face. The spray would burn its eyes and nose. The jackal runs away. The polecat resumes looking for its own meal. Thanks to its smelly trick, it will survive another night.

Elephants communicate with each other using smells from saliva, urine, and fluids made from glands in their bodies.

Surviving with Smells

Animals face many challenges. They must find places to live and avoid predators that want to eat them. To have young, many animals must seek out **mates**. Animals use many tools to survive. Smell is often one of those tools.

Smells can be helpful. Animals can use smells to send messages to enemies or mates. Odors can chase animals away or attract them.

Explore Online

Visit the website below. What new information did you learn about how animals use scent that wasn't in Chapter One?

Chemical Communication

abdocorelibrary.com/getting-smelly -to-survive

Skunks are able to shoot
their smelly spray up to
10 to 20 feet (3–6 m).

CHAPTER 2

STINK ATTACK

The most famous animal that fights off predators using smell is probably the skunk. Several **species** of skunks live in the Americas. There are striped, spotted, hooded, and hog-nosed skunks. All skunks really know how to stink.

A skunk gives a warning before it stinks things up. If predators ignore the black-and-white warning colors on a skunk's fur, the skunk may stamp its feet. The skunk can twist to aim its rear at the danger. Any predator sticking around gets a smelly blast from glands in the skunk's rear.

Beetle Spray

Bombardier beetles live under logs and leaf litter. These beetles are found all around the world. The bugs are small but mighty.

The beetle stores **chemicals** inside its guts. If a predator attacks, the beetle quickly mixes the chemicals together. The chemicals blow up. Then, a hot, stinky liquid shoots out of the beetle's rear end.

Inside a Bombardier Beetle

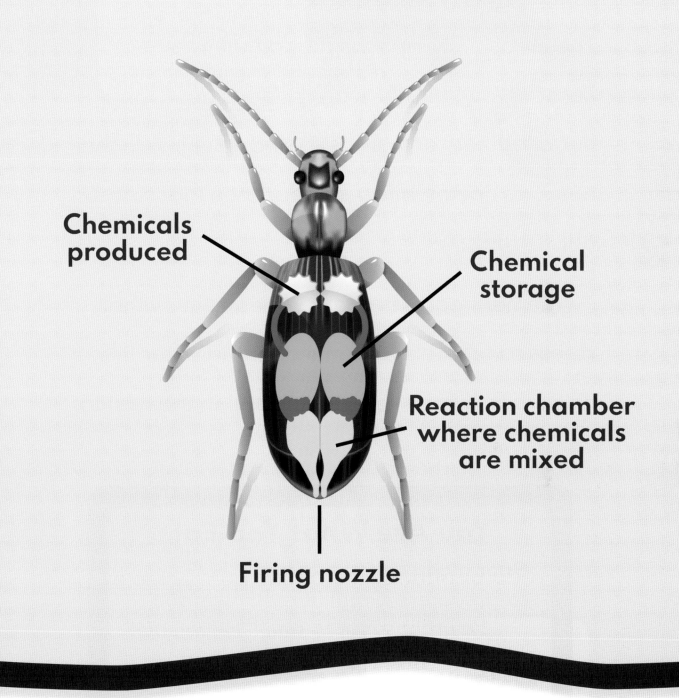

Chemicals produced

Chemical storage

Reaction chamber where chemicals are mixed

Firing nozzle

This diagram shows how bombardier beetles get smelly. The beetles can shoot 500 blasts of liquid in a second.

Poopy Protection

The Eurasian hoopoe is a bird that lives in Europe, Asia, and Africa. Hoopoes have long head feathers and striped wings. But inside their nests, it's not the birds' appearance that stands out. It's the smell.

Mother hoopoes coat their eggs in oil that smells rotten. This oil fights bacteria. After the chicks hatch, they keep their poop in the nest to

You Are What You Eat

Odor alone can't protect skunks from all predators. Great horned owls don't have a great sense of smell. In fact, the birds find skunks to be a tasty meal. As a result, great horned owls sometimes smell of skunk.

A mother Eurasian hoopoe feeds her chicks.

use as a weapon. Predators that find the chicks get a face full of stinky poop. The chicks also spray liquid poop from their rears at predators!

Further Evidence

Look at the website below. Does it give any new evidence to support Chapter Two?

Why Do Skunks Stink?

abdocorelibrary.com/getting-smelly
-to-survive

Adult tigers range from 6 to 10 feet (1.8–3 m) long. They can weigh 220 to 660 pounds (100–300 kg).

CHAPTER 3

HOME, SMELLY HOME

Animals need places to feed and find mates. Some kinds of animals claim an area as their **territory**. Animals can't hang up signs to mark their land, but they can leave scent marks.

A male tiger marks his territory.

Tiger Territory

Tigers are the largest of the wild cats. Only a few thousand of them remain in Asia. Big animals need lots of food. Tigers need territories with a large population of prey animals.

To guard their territory, the cats use smells. Scent glands make their pee and poop smellier. They pee on trees and leafy branches. Tigers also have scent glands on their faces. They rub these scent glands on objects. When other tigers smell the marks, they know to stay away.

Cat Rubs

Like tigers, house cats have scent glands on their faces. Cats often rub their scents on objects in a home. Cats will also use their faces to apply scents to other creatures they live with, including humans.

Red-backed salamanders make their homes under logs on the forest floor.

Salamander Spaces

Red-backed salamanders live in the forests of eastern North America. They dine on small animals such as insects and snails. The salamanders breathe through their skin, so they need to stay wet.

Red-backed salamanders live under rocks and logs. The ground under these objects doesn't dry out quickly. The salamanders mark their territory with scent glands under their tails.

PRIMARY SOURCE

Ratan Lal Brahmachary is a scientist who works with tiger scents. While explaining why it was important to save tigers as a species, he said:

> How can I study tigers if the tiger [dies out] before completing my studies?

Source: Ratan Lal Brahmachary. "The Smelly World of Tiger Pheromones." *Nature India*, 11 Dec. 2014, natureasia.com. Accessed 18 Nov. 2021.

Point of View

What is the speaker's point of view on this topic? What is your point of view? Write a short essay about how they are similar and different.

A female spongy moth on an oak tree

CHAPTER 4

ANIMAL PERFUME

Not all animal smells are meant to drive others away. Some are meant to attract others. Getting smelly is one way for an animal to find a mate.

A female spongy moth stays in a tree. To get a mate, she gives off a powerful smell.

A spongy moth larva feasts on a tree leaf.

A male follows the scent to find her. After mating, the female lays eggs on her tree. After the **larvae** hatch, the tree leaves will provide them with plenty of food to eat.

Smelly Pest Control

The smell of spongy moths can be used against them. People add fake female scent to moth traps. Males who go to the traps can't mate with females. Females who can't find mates don't lay eggs.

Adult male musk oxen typically weigh about 700 pounds (320 kg).

A Pleasant Stink

Musk oxen are hairy herd animals that live on plains in the Arctic. Their name comes from the earthy smell the males produce. They mate only during a time called the rut. This happens during the late summer.

Male musk oxen fight each other for mates during the rut.

During the rut, males fight each other for females. Sometimes they crash into each other with their heads. The males also make themselves stink. They produce a strong-smelling pee. Some of it gets on their fur. This scent attracts female musk oxen looking to mate. Along with warm fur and a hard head, smell is another tool a musk ox uses to survive.

Many animals, such as alligators, use potent scents to attract mates.

> Alligators eject a jet of powerful scent from glands under their jaws to attract their mates. During the spring breeding season, this odorous vapor hangs over an alligator swamp like a fog.

Source: Ilo Hiller. "Chemical Communication." *Young Naturalist*, n.d. tpwd.texas.gov. Accessed 21 Dec. 2021.

What's the Big Idea?

Read this quote carefully. What is its main idea? Explain how the main idea is supported by details.

SURVIVAL FACTS

Animals use smells in many different ways to help them survive.

A prey animal may get smelly to drive off a predator.

Scent markers help an animal claim a territory so it does not have to share space and food.

Some animals use smells to help them get mates.

Glossary

chemicals
substances with certain properties

glands
parts of an animal that make or let out chemicals

larvae
young, wingless forms of many insects that hatch
from eggs

mate
an animal that comes together with another animal of the
same species to have young

predator
an animal that lives by killing and eating other animals

species
a group of similar living things that can have
young together

territory
an area that is marked and defended by a particular type
of animal

Online Resources

To learn more about getting smelly to survive, visit our free resource websites below.

Visit **abdocorelibrary.com** or scan this QR code for free Common Core resources for teachers and students, including vetted activities, multimedia, and booklinks, for deeper subject comprehension.

Visit **abdobooklinks.com** or scan this QR code for free additional online weblinks for further learning. These links are routinely monitored and updated to provide the most current information available.

Learn More

Eamer, Claire. *Extremely Gross Animals: Stinky, Slimy and Strange Animal Adaptations*. Kids Can, 2021.

Pringle, Laurence. *The Secret Life of the Skunk*. Boyds Mills, 2019.

Index

About the Author

Clara MacCarald is a freelance writer with a master's degree in ecology and natural resources. She lives with her family in an off-grid house nestled in the forests of central New York. When not parenting her daughter, she spends her time writing nonfiction books for kids.